BLUFF Y...

CONSULTANCY

NIGEL VINEY

RR

RAVETTE BOOKS

Published by Ravette Books Limited
Egmont House
8 Clifford Street
London WC1X 1RB
Tel & Fax: (01 0403) 711443

First printed 1986
Reprinted 1989, 1991 ,1992, 1993, 1994

Series Editor – Anne Tauté

Cover design – Jim Wire
Printing & binding – Cox & Wyman Ltd.
Production – Oval Projects Ltd.

The Bluffer's Guides® is a
Registered Trademark.

The Bluffer's Guides® series is based
on an original idea by Peter Wolfe.

An Oval Project
for Ravette Books Ltd.

CONTENTS

The Image 7
  Consultancy 7
  Publicity 8
  Self-Promotion 9
  Appearance 10
  Transport 13
  A Personal Chauffeur 14
  Stationery 16
  An Office 17
  Equipment 18

Rules of the Game 19
  Making a Date 19
  Fixing a Time 20
  Playing Hard to Get 21
  The First Meeting 22
  Entertaining 23
  Fees 24
  Payment 26
  Invoicing 27
  Friends 29

Tactics 30
  Objectives 30
  Research 31
  Secrecy and Code-words 32
  Jargon 33
  Making Use of Networks 34
  Meetings 36
  Table-turning 38
  Dealing with People 39

Going Overseas   40
The Importance of Anecdotes   43

Specialist Consultants   45

Recommendations   47

The Report   58
Appearance   58
Size   59
Quantity   59
Contents   60
Embellishments   60
Essentials   61

INTRODUCTION

When you meet someone today who says "I am a consultant", you will very probably suppose that he or she is in fact, unemployed. These days the middle classes do not retire, nor are they made redundant or given the sack. Rather than claiming to be in any of these distressing conditions, the middle classes become, or perhaps say that they have become, consultants. "It's extraordinary," they tell you, lying in their teeth, "I'm busier than ever."

Consultancy has become, then, a euphemism for the state of being unemployed. This book is not for such people, who have brought consultancy a bad name. It is for those who actually seek to earn a living from consultancy, without knowing the smallest thing about it. In other words, for bluffers.

Fortunately, the twin conditions of bluffing and of consultancy are largely synonymous. It is not just that the skills required in these two jobs overlap, it is that the skills are in fact the same in both trades. Being a consultant means being an expert in a field which you have yourself invented, namely that of telling people who have been doing a job for years, that you know how to do that job better. A bluffer is somebody who pretends to do all this, which comes to very much the same thing in the end.

Both are in the position of the racing tipster. It is, of course, an absurdity to make a living by publishing daily racing tips in a newspaper when, if you were really any good at the job, you would keep the tips strictly to yourself and make a fortune. Telling anybody else what you intend to back would simply shorten the odds, and reduce the amount of money you would make. So it is with consultants. If they really were any good at running a business they would be off somewhere doing it, instead of purporting to tell others how to do it.

You may comfort yourself with the fact that there is never a time when people do not want to be told. Indeed, one of the glories of the consultant's trade lies in the timing of the availability of work. For the oddity is that the consultant is more in demand in bad times than in good.

If things should happen to be going well, and the business is prospering, it rarely occurs to those in charge to look around for ways to make things go even better. Falling profits, not to speak of losses, on the other hand, are always a signal to call in the consultant.

Bad times in the business world are by no means bad times, therefore, for us. Consultancy flourishes in bad times. While you cannot exactly create these conditions, you should be able to concentrate your effort in trades which are in the throes of a recession. If retailing is booming, leave retailing alone. Go elsewhere and find a nice healthy slump.

THE IMAGE

Consultancy

The original concept of consultancy was invented by doctors, not much more than one hundred years ago. It is highly significant that doctors in those days were bluffers to a man (and some would say that some of them are to this day). The consultant physicians and surgeons were simply bigger, better and more successful bluffers than the rest of the profession.

The real stars, the super-bluffers, were the consultants at teaching hospitals in chauffeur-driven Rolls-Royces (or their horse-drawn equivalent in the earlier days). The door was opened for them by the Head Porter, bowing low. They sailed up the steps in a stately fashion, eventually emerging into the wards followed by long processions of underlings and assistants.

They put on a tremendous act. They terrorised nurses, students, registrars, house-physicians, sisters and *even* matrons. They were especially good at terrorising patients. Not having much in the way of drugs, nor very much knowledge, they simply terrorised patients into recovery. Or not, as the case might be.

The present-day practicioner of bluffing does well to study these great pioneers. Many of them made large fortunes, which is something which all true bluffers will wish to emulate. The would-be consultant moreover, has the great advantage of not having to pass any tedious examinations during the apprenticeship. Indeed, there is no apprenticeship.

The bluffer decides to be a consultant, and is one, then and there.

Publicity

The biggest problem for the consultant is not, as might be supposed by the uninitiated, how to *do* the job – how to put into effect the monstrous impudence of telling experienced people how to do their work. This book sets out in detail how to deal with this aspect of the consultant's affairs. There is no difficulty.

The real difficulty comes earlier. How do you get yourself consulted? How do you get somebody to ask you to do something or other? How do you create the situation where captains of industry will turn to you, a cry of distress on their lips and flourishing a chequebook?

The answer to these questions will occur readily enough to a true consultant, since the answer lies in an art with which all aspirants should be familiar. The art is writing fiction. The consultant has to establish a **reputation**, starting from zero. If you have recently been fired from a job, you can be said to be starting from below zero. A reputation has to be created.

Every industry, not to speak of management itself, has several publications devoted to it, weekly, monthly, or whatever. Some of these journals are learned, some are sensational; all are excruciatingly boring. The editors of these publications, harassed and underpaid for the most part, have the same problems as any editors, whether of daily papers or parish magazines – how to fill up the space between the advertisements without spending too much money. You can greatly help these poor persons by providing an article, or a series of articles, either at a very low rate of payment or even free. Do this with good grace, since what you are actually doing is providing yourself with a series of advertisements for yourself and your alleged services.

Each article must be introduced with a short and boastful paragraph about yourself and a photograph. Care must be taken with this picture. Although it can be created in a do-it-yourself booth in Woolworths, it must have a credit line of a glamorous-sounding but fictional photographer. 'Photograph by d'Angoulême, Paris' for example, or 'Photograph: Ricci, New York'.

All articles will tell the story of some past, but imaginary, triumph – how you were able to 'diagnose the problems of a company,' and how you were able to 'recommend changes' which soon led to 'vastly increased profits.'

Fortunately a bluffer is able, indeed is compelled, early in each article, to make a po-faced declaration to the effect that a consultant must, above all things, be discreet, as though you had signed a species of Hippocratic Oath, which inhibits you from the naming of names, and revealing who your clients are or were. This gives confidence to those thinking of employing you, while giving full scope to your imagination.

Self-Promotion

The newly-launched consultant must study the art of **self-promotion**. Here your model should be the late Field Marshal Montgomery, who was a superb performer in the art of forcing people to notice him and to remember him. He was utterly unlike any General before him, and deliberately so. As Monty developed his image in the Western Desert in 1942 with the skilled aid of a photographer (Captain Geoffrey Keating), so too, should a consultant enlist the aid of a snapper.

Have yourself photographed doing things which will

make you remembered, and have them published in the trade press. Sponsored parachute jumps are a possibility, though such energetic activities are not obligatory. You could, for example, borrow a bicycle and be photographed chaining it to railings outside the Bank of England. The caption can be innocuous, but the picture suggests, subliminally perhaps, close contact with the powers-that-be in the City.

Another possibility is to be photographed arriving at an office with a dog. Any old dog will not do. A peke on a lead has implications which no one will relish. An ill-behaved dog is counter-productive. The ideal animal is a superbly-trained gun-dog which simply walks quietly along beside you, stops when you do, lies in a corner when directed there with a gesture, and only gets up at another signal. This sort of dog suggests total competence. By association, it suggests that the consultant is competent in all things.

Other animals are not recommended. A cheetah on a lead, a parrot on a shoulder, a white mouse in a pocket are all equally undesirable. On the other hand, arrival on horseback, in the right circumstances, can be a sensationally effective method of self-promotion.

Appearance

A vital part of your career as a successful consultant is to **seem different**. At all times appear to be, to clients, a creature from another world; better, more profitable, better-organised and perhaps more glamorous. An important part of the process of seeming to be different, perhaps the most important part, lies in dressing altogether differently.

For example, one consultant in industry in the

1950's understood this very well. In those days all business men dressed uniformly, like Russians, in suits, white shirts and ties. A bow-tie was an extreme gesture, equivalent today to a purple Mohican haircut. Even suede shoes were suspect. It was of course true that minute and subtle differences between one man and the next could be discerned by those interested in such matters. The cut of the suit, the nature of the shirt, the quality and pattern of the tie, even the socks could and did tell a tale.

Michael R. ignored such mundane distinctions. He invariably dressed very formally, out-dressing everyone in sight. He wore a short black coat, striped trousers, stiff collar and a black tie. This garb was then the normal everyday wear of Cabinet Ministers, Permanent Secretaries, judges, barristers and, most significantly, senior consultants in London teaching hospitals. His clothes consequently established him, to businessmen, as somebody from a different and superior world. Before he opened his mouth, he already seemed to be a man of power and authority.

Slavish following of this admirable technique is not recommended today. Apart from barristers, whose uniform this get-up still remains, the style is so unusual that it runs the risk of being mistaken for fancy-dress. Styles of clothes in offices are different today and the technique must be adapted accordingly, but bow-ties remain a very good idea.

Wearing strange hats is an outdated ploy now that the wearing of hats is in itself strange; consequently any hat will suit the purpose. Funny waistcoats can be helpful, but their alleged provenance must be well thought out in advance. "Waistcoat? Oh yes, a gift from the Queen of Siam." As in all things, a measure of restraint must be the consultant's motto.

In some places, of course, suits and ties are still de rigueur. In others, ties are unheard of, and jeans and jogging-shoes predominate. What you should do is to reconnoitre carefully, establish what the normal wear is in the office you will be visiting, and then **wear the opposite**. If the place is one of the informal, laid-back variety, then dress with reasonable formality. If it is a bank or an insurance company, or anywhere in which anything like the style of thirty years ago remains, then turn up in a stylish track-suit and trainers.

To make sure of the facts, it will be necessary for you to spend an hour or two in the neighbourhood, in disguise, to check out the appearance of future clients. Sit in a parked car in a convenient place, perhaps in the firm's car park, wearing dark glasses and making notes. In this way you will be virtually invisible. If noticed at all, it will simply be supposed that you are a salesperson wasting some other company's time. You need not go to the trouble and expense of disguising yourself as a street-sweeper to effect this reconnaissance: street-sweepers are so rare as to be highly conspicuous.

There is an alternative method of dressing, which has the great advantage of appearing different in all types of offices. The outstanding merit of this approach lies in the fact that it enables you to visit offices of varying types in one day without resorting to quick-changes in public lavatories. The trick is to dress as a farmer. A robust appearance is an advantage, but the essence of the matter is thick tweeds, Newmarket checks, heavy brogue shoes, and the manner of one who has just come in from the milking. Added props can include a deer-stalker hat (with or without fishing flies in it), a crook, a sheep-dog and a button-hole. Straw attached to the person, or a smell of manure is going too far.

Transport

Just as the assiduous and successful consultant must dress with care and attention to detail, so too must he or she take pains to arrive at the client's offices in proper style. This naturally matters most in places where the company car park is clearly visible from the offices.

You must take great pains to avoid up-staging your client with your car. To most business people the car, which of course means the company's car, is not only a supreme status symbol; it is also symbolic of the individual's own power and authority, and even relates to sexual prowess, a concept which has been in existence since Ben Hur invented the idea that speed and virility were very closely linked.

Consequently, if you know that the man you are to meet drives a Mercedes, on no account hire a Rolls for the day when going to visit him. Nor should you ever arrive in the sort of car which the company awards to its junior salesmen. A consultant must seem to be both powerful and successful, but not in a manner which in any way puts the client down. As with clothes, careful reconnaissance is required.

Expert bluffers will readily apprehend that, in many respects, a vintage car would be a very suitable vehicle: such a car threatens nobody, is manifestly different from all the other cars in the company car park, and is neither cheap nor common.

Another answer to the problem is a sports car. No company would dream of providing such cars for any grade of its staff. They do not figure in the company-car pecking order. They are different; they are expensive. In other words, sports cars are ideal in every way. But be careful: a Ferrari is probably too ostentatious; a BMW would be best, perhaps. It massages the client's ego when he comes to realise that you, a successful and forward-looking consultant, a BMW driver no less, will be doing his dirty work for him.

In cities these considerations are less compelling. If there is any chance that your client will actually see you arrive or depart, then the procedure is simple – you hire a suitable car and driver for the day, and leave it parked, preferably on a double-yellow line outside the front door.

But these are rare necessities, since in city centres your arrival and departure are almost always unwitnessed. So the sensible thing to do is to travel by bicycle. The only difficulty here is the problem of making the point that a bicycle has been used at all. Two courses are open to you. Forget to remove your bicycle clips until you reach the client's own office, or carry a pump and a front light in your hand. Alternatively, and more emphatically, use a collapsible and folding bike, and take it right up and into the client's office, parking it under the hat-stand. This ploy is greatly to be recommended in any sort of sky-scraper, particularly in health-conscious New York.

A Personal Chauffeur

Should a situation demand frequent visits to an office in a city centre, you will undoubtedly be faced with a car-parking problem. Experts will recognise an easy way of overcoming this problem.

It will not have escaped your eagle eye, going about your lawful occasions, that various categories of cars and other vehicles are in practice immune from parking restrictions, apparently invisible to the warden's eye. Cars belonging to the disabled, doctors' cars and diplomatic cars are well-known examples, but not areas for the bluffer to meddle in. Plumbers' vans are in a similar position, but these are not recommended owing to the subsequent difficulty of establishing credibility, not to speak of the poor jokes which might arise ('Come to stop the leaks here? Ho-ho-ho'). The area to exploit is the chauffeur-driven car, similarly immune from the traffic-warden's tickets.

It is suprisingly easy to have what appears to be a chauffeur-driven car without going to the trouble and expense of actually employing a chauffeur. The way to do this is to have (literally) a dummy chauffeur. To get hold of an inflatable human figure, you will be obliged to fill in a mail-order form in a dubious magazine. You must then acquire, or hire, a chauffeur's uniform of a suitable size for the dummy. This is not as simple as it sounds, since the only human inflatable figures available are aggressively female in shape. Some sort of breast-reducing operation may have to be performed, and a puncture-repair outfit brought into use.

It is acknowledged that the best technique is to keep the figure, ready inflated and uniformed, in the boot of the car, rather than inflating it as required. All you then have to do is to force the figure into position in the driving seat, with the car already parked.

One of the great advantages of this simple ruse lies in its effect on the client. If he is deceived, as the traffic warden will be deceived, he will be suitably impressed by the fact that you have a chauffeur. If, on the other hand, the client happens to look out of the window when you are wrestling the figure into position, or extracting it and putting it away in the boot, he will be bound to be overcome with admiration for your ingenuity.

15

Stationery

The wise consultant will devote much care and attention to personal stationery. A modest investment here will pay handsome dividends, since stationery puts in an appearance early in the relationship with clients, and the wrong sort of writing paper or business card can mar an otherwise promising situation.

Nothing flashy is to be considered. Just because the consultant is a fully-paid-up smart-alec, his stationery, indeed his whole demeanour, must suggest that he is nothing of the kind. Consequently letterheads must hint at good breeding, and suggest solidity and genuine worth.

It does not do to get too carried away when examining a book of specimen letterheads. The old-world atmosphere can easily be overdone. A telegraphic address is a good possibility. It can naturally be fictional, since nobody is going to send you a tele-message. But the wording, if chosen with care, can be a help in promoting your image. Something like 'Profitability, London' would do very well. To precede these words with a small picture of a telegraph pole would be an error of judgement. Cards are worth a similar degree of trouble and here again the first consideration is to avoid flashiness. Restrict yourself to the normal size, and not a piece of pasteboard the size of a five-pound note which is favoured by the French. Use only one colour ink, preferably black. It is a good plan to have a Japanese or an Arabic translation on the reverse side of the card. Modest ability in sleight-of-hand and constant practise will ensure that you invariably present the card translation-side up.

It is essential to resist a natural impulse to make up the Arabic or the Japanese script by copying something off a packet in a supermarket. This would be to neglect those tiresome people who can actually make head or tail of outlandish alphabets.

Never forget the story of a handsome and distinguished-looking old lady, elegantly turned out, who often wore an attractive brass disc hanging on a chain around her neck. On the disc were some Chinese characters. The effect was charming. Having found the artefact in a junk-shop, she wore it for years, until an unhappy day when she encountered a former Shanghai policeman at a cocktail-party who was brutal enough, or tactless enough, to tell her that the characters spelt out 'Licensed Prostitute Number 138'.

The Office

True consultants never have offices of their own. They are very well aware of the tax-effectiveness of working from home, where, no doubt, they may well have a room devoted to their consulting activities. All that is required in this room is a table and a chair, with a word processor and an answer-phone.

You should not yourself record the message on the tape which tells the caller you will be available shortly, and so on. It should be recorded by a friend. This heightens the impression that you are both busy and important. Furthermore it suggests that you have an organisation behind you. As it is generally secretaries who will make phone calls to you, and as they are only impressed by other secretaries, it is no more than prudent to arrange matters to sound as though there is a secretary working for you. Thus, when making calls, you should cultivate a skill in mimicry, making the call in one voice, preferably female, and then handing it on so to speak, to yourself.

It is usually thought reasonable for your clients to provide you with an office. But be careful to ensure that you are not provided with a glorified cupboard for this purpose. It is essential that the office be a reasonable one, as you will not be treated seriously if it is not. Offices and their fittings are the commercial equivalent of badges of rank in the services – visible indicators of status. See that yours is above average.

Equipment

Never use a clip-board. If a note has to be made, it should be done by writing a single word in a slim pocket book.

A briefcase is no part of the true consultant's equipment either. They have become absurd affairs, and are today what the newly-joined junior employees carry their lunchtime sandwiches about in. For this reason alone they are to be sternly avoided as ill befitting the image which you are taking such pains to establish.

It does happen, however, that you are constrained to take some papers about with you. The best thing to do is to fold them up and put them in a pocket. One top-class bluffing consultant who adopts the style and appearance of a country squire, has poacher's pockets made in his baggy tweed suits for this very purpose.

If, however, there are too many papers to be carried about in this fashion, then select one of the following preferred and recommended methods:

1. a Sainsbury's carrier bag
2. a canvas hold-all
3. an ancient leather attaché-case, covered in faded hotel labels from the 1930's.
4. a Gladstone bag.

RULES OF THE GAME

Making a Date

When arranging to meet a client it is very useful to have a good diary, filled with information about public events. This is most important if prospective clients are being approached. Experienced consultants will at once understand the value of being able to say something on the lines of: "What about next Tuesday? Unless, of course you are going to be at Ascot. . ."

This up-staging technique has twin advantages. On the one hand it implies that the client is rich enough, powerful enough and important enough to be at Ascot. It implies that he or she has, or has access to, a private box there. There are flattering overtones of lobsters, champagne and strawberries. On the other hand, it suggests that you would be there too if other more important events, such as the meeting being planned, had not arisen. In this way it is hinted that the consultant is part of the social scene; all that is implied for the flatteree is automatically implied for the flatterer as well.

Royal Garden Parties are the best possible events for this ploy. Mid-week sporting events may be used, but this has to be done with skill and discretion. The June, or Royal, Ascot Meeting is acceptable, but not other meetings. Test matches at Lord's are in order; Goodwood in July, a possibility. The Oval Test Match is to be avoided, as are Wimbledon and The Derby, and not merely because they occur south of the Thames; they are all too popular to be flattering. It can readily be seen, therefore, that Henley Regatta is an occasion which can be used with great confidence. The Open (golf) is up to snuff for the purpose, and the

University Rugger Match at Twickenham is a perfect choice.

If you have a truly comprehensive diary guard against getting carried away by the wealth of information it contains. Exclusiveness is a fine thing, but it should not be taken to the point of mentioning events which are so exclusive that spectators are barely visible. Croquet at Hurlingham, archery at Holyrood Palace, frisbee championships and so on, are to be avoided.

French horse races, with all the implications of private jets, extreme wealth and chic, would be the best possible events for the purpose, were it not for the fact that they occur on Sundays; but, even here there are occasions when knowledge of the date of 'The Arc' might be useful.

Fixing a Time

When a day has been fixed for a meeting, the time has to be agreed. Always take the initiative at this point. Suggest a time which is long before the client would dream of arriving at his office, or long after he or she normally departs.

As always, time spent in reconnaissance will not have been wasted. If you know quite well that the person you're talking to usually turns up at about 9.30, it is sound practice to say "Would 8.30 be too early?" If he or she is normally out of the office like a bullet at 5.30, then ask "Would 7 o'clock suit you? I ought to be able to manage that. . ."

It is not at all a bad idea to start this dialogue by suggesting meeting on a Saturday or a Sunday, using **the date**. If the client expostulates "But that's a

Saturday", you respond "Of course!" in surprised and slightly pained tones.

All this, of course, is designed to establish you as an extraordinarily assiduous individual. It suggests that the client is busy, important and hard-working when he may well be none of these. It is intimidating, in the subtlest possible way.

It may be that the client turns out to be a person of sense, who will in no way tolerate this kind of nonsense. He will name a time himself. In this case, you should never accept the first time offered. Play hard to get. Use phrases such as "I have a meeting that afternoon, but I can probably get it postponed . . ." and "Unfortunately I see that my plane does not land until. . ."

As well as seeming to be different, a creature from another world, you must always seem, especially with potential clients, to be engaged in many other, and enormously important projects. As discretion is acknowledged to be important, nobody is likely to ask you what you are actually up to – and if anyone does have the temerity to cross-question you, then you can make it plain that the cross-questioner is breaking one of the rules.

Playing Hard to Get

A well-known restaurant was opened some twenty years ago in King's Road, in London. It has now spread and has several branches and satellite establishments.

When it first opened, it was the aim of its Italian-born owners to make it as desirable as possible, from its inception; to make it the most sought-after place in town. To achieve this they adopted a bold scheme.

Although opened ostensibly with a mass of publicity, there were for the first three weeks no staff in the place, except for one man who answered the telephone and dealt with the front door. His job was simple. He told everybody who rang up, or called at the door, that the place was fully booked that day and for the next two weeks, and then took a booking for some date not less than three weeks ahead.

As a result when the restaurant really opened, fully staffed and ready for business, it was in fact fully booked. And since it served excellent food, it has remained busy to this day.

The impish proprietors had exploited with resounding success the human foible which supposes that anything popular must be a success, and the equally human feeling that anything unobtainable, or hard to obtain, is desirable.

For a consultant to adopt the same policy would border on the fool-hardy. But the message should be borne in mind. Always be hard to get. A blank diary must be made to seem full. Bogus meetings must be cancelled or postponed. You must always appear to have had to tear yourself away from urgent and important matters to attend to your client's needs.

The First Meeting

Business potentates, either real or imagined, have a passion for unnecessary secrecy. Many of them are skilled at and greatly enjoy, intrigue. It is advisable for you to bear these foibles in mind, and to join in the cloak-and-dagger game if it seems appropriate.

If the client says, when fixing a first meeting, "Now, how can we meet?" be quick to recognise that for some reason the client does not want a consultant to come to his office. It may very well be, in fact it is highly probable, that the client is deeply involved in an office war, in which you may soon be involved; but at present the client wishes to keep your existence to himself, as it were, for later use as a secret weapon.

You should play along, and reply positively to what is almost bound to be nonsense. Arrange a meeting for breakfast, naming the most expensive place you can think of for the purpose. In London, for example, suggest breakfast at The Connaught.

While doing your best to feed the client's appetite for secrecy, don't get carried away. Locations for semi-clandestine meetings should be practical, not exotic. To suggest meeting at, say, the third bench on the left walking up The Broad Walk smacks altogether too much of John le Carré. In any case, there is no breakfast to be had there, and the least a consultant should expect for pandering to such behaviour is a square meal.

Entertaining

Never, on any account, entertain a client, still less a potential client. It is manifestly the business of the client to entertain the consultant. In being entertained, however, it is important for you to bear in mind the overriding need for a consultant to seem different. In this context, therefore, it means different from the people a client normally expects to entertain. The consultant must never do the expected thing, or pursue the ordinary course down the ordinary groove.

If you are being taken out to lunch, you may be sure that this is primarily because your host wishes to give himself a decent meal. Secondly, he probably wishes to beguile you at the same time. This transparent manoeuvre is best countered by always doing the unlikely thing.

If the host offers a drink, insist on mineral water, iced and with a slice of lemon in it. If the host suggests lobster, or other expensive luxuries, choose the cheapest thing on the menu. If there is nothing cheap on the menu, the best thing to do is to request an omelette and a plain salad, or some steamed fish. If the host stuffs himself with a huge meal, you should austerely omit the middle course.

The probability will be that the whole lunch will be exceedingly boring. True consultants know the way to deal with this situation. They glance at their watch. It should not be done constantly as this is likely to give offence. It should be done once only, and decisively. Then you should say you are very sorry to have to break off this fascinating discussion but a car is coming to pick you up in five minutes to take you to the airport, since you have to be in Zurich by seven o'clock.

On no account worry about being spotted not getting into a car, but sauntering away to the nearest bus-stop. Your lunch-time companion will be sitting peacefully at the table, comforting himself with the reflection that it will be in order for two double-brandies to appear on the bill.

Fees

The size of **the fee** which you will charge is naturally a matter of supreme importance. Never make a rushed decision. Take time to feel your way into the situation, and to assess what the traffic will bear.

Never mention a fee at the first meeting; instead ask all the questions you can think of; make enigmatic remarks about the interest the problem arouses; ponder visibly and deeply, and nod wisely. If the client raises the matter at this first meeting and asks how much the consultancy is going to cost, turn a shade haughty in demeanour and reply that any assessment of costs must naturally depend upon the **preliminary appraisal.** It is also sound tactics at this point to prepare the client a little with a throw-away line about 'consultancy at this level' never being cheap.

When you have had the chance to do some preliminary sniffing around, you must raise the question of the fee yourself. It is vital that this is done face-to-face with the responsible client, since you will of course push the fee as far up as you can, and the client's reactions are an essential part of this process. The opening gambit should be on the lines of: "My normal fee is six hundred dollars a day." (Fees should always be quoted in foreign currencies, because this often makes the fee sound less than it really is, and is in any case more impressive. Swiss francs and American dollars are the most favoured currencies for this purpose.)

Watch closely to see the reaction to your opening statement. If the client blenches visibly, gulps, blinks, or changes colour markedly, and provided you need the job badly, you should add: "But of course, for something of this nature, which is going to go for several weeks, the fee can come down a bit – to something nearer five hundred dollars."

If, on the other hand, the client shows no sign of concern, you add in the other direction, as it were, "Plus **expenses**, of course, and **research assistance** which will probably not amount to more than two hundred and fifty dollars – say nine hundred dollars a day in round figures – provided, naturally, that an office and secretarial assistance are going to be provided." This sort of catalogue can be continued almost indefinitely, but you must watch carefully all the time you're spilling it out, and cut it off at the first vestige of a hint of trouble.

Never underplay your hand. It is important to remember that everybody knows and expects consultancy to be an expensive business. Nobody should be disillusioned in this matter.

Of course, if the man sitting there had any sense he would tell you what the fee is; but then, naturally, he would not be the sort of person who resorts to consultants in any case.

Payment

It occasionally happens that the bluffing consultant is obliged to work, or rather to charge for his work, by the hour. The all-important question, plainly, is how much to charge for each hour worked. At this point it is very helpful to be aware of the normal number of hours worked by the ordinary employee on an annual salary.

Assuming, for office work, a 9.30 to 5.30 working day and allowing for an hour off at lunchtime, ignoring tea and coffee breaks, and assuming a five-day week, you arrive at a figure of 35 hours a week. A full year at this rate yields 1820 hours. But 140 hours must be deducted to take care of an annual four-week holiday allotment, leaving 1680 hours. From this figure again, 42 hours have to be taken for the eight statutory days of Bank Holidays enjoyed by those who work in England and Scotland. This leaves 1638 hours. From this figure, yet again, it is reasonable to deduct another week away from work to allow for odd days off for sickness, minor ailments, having to stay in all day waiting for the gas-man and other domestic hitches which are, in the nature of things, bound to occur during the year.

In other words, the ordinary office worker actually puts in about 1600 hours every year. Therefore somebody earning £12,000 a year is being paid at the rate of £7.50 an hour. But accountants have a rule of thumb which postulates that the real cost of employing a person (allowing for National Insurance, pension contributions and so on) is 25 per cent above the cash figure. Thus somebody being paid £12,000 a year is actually costing his employers £15,000, so that the real rate of pay of the £12,000 a year man is more like £10.00 an hour. And this figure takes no account of any **overheads** – notional cost of the square footage occupied, telephone costs, heating, lighting and so on. . .

These sums are useful to a consultant in assessing charges. They are also useful if your hourly charge of, say, £50.00 an hour is queried as exorbitant. All you have to do is ask the querier to calculate his or her own salary, or their secretaries', on this basis. The results are invariably salutary.

Invoicing

Many years ago a wise old printer used to say that when he was quoting for jobs he made it his practice to ensure that figures quoted by his firm were not in round numbers. Odd shillings and pence, even the half-pence then in use, were arbitrarily added or subtracted. This, he used to say, lent verisimilitude. Nobody could suspect that a figure of, say, £182.17.4d had not been worked out in the most precise detail. It gave confidence in the way that a figure of £180.0s.0d. could not.

Bluffers should bear this technique in mind. Round numbers can be suspect, and should be avoided. Furthermore, you should take pains to split your invoices as much as possible. Invoices should be presented monthly, and it is always a good plan to invoice expenses separately from fees. This has the benefit of seeming to reduce the overall total.

Be well aware too, that any payment in kind is enormously valuable. Secretarial back-up, the use of a telephone, use of copying machines (or in-house printing facilities), a company petrol pump, office meals, office drinks – all these, and other services, are valuable in aggregate and have the great advantage of appearing to cost the client nothing.

A skilled consultant of the recent past, George C., used to exploit these services to the extent of actually moving into his client's offices, and taking up his abode there during the time he was carrying out, or rather appearing to carry out, his consultancy duties. He always maintained that it was a comfortable way of life, quite apart from being economical. If the office he was working in did not actually have sleeping accommodation, there were always plenty of comfortable sofas about, not to speak of central heating and masses of hot water. Whether or not he revealed his temporary place of residence to his clients, he did not choose to say.

Friends

Once you have set up as a consultant, you will begin to find that there are plenty of people around who will seek to match your own ingenuity. You will very soon discover that one of your most intractable problems is the old friend, or would-be old friend, who is after free advice.

These people are pernicious, and it goes without saying that their efforts must be defeated at all costs. They will seek out the consultant, trading on some past acquaintanceship, or cashing in on the spurious camaradarie of the club bar, or other such place. They will try to entertain you with lavish lunches, pour liquor into you in an effort to loosen your tongue, and endeavour to pick your brains.

We all have friends. They can hardly be avoided. But this is a desperate situation, and the consultant must take a stern line. You are recommended to adopt the following courses:

a) resign from all clubs, and similar organizations where you are liable to meet potential clients on terms of social amiability.

b) never accept invitations to lunch, except from existing clients.

c) if somebody calls, with honeyed phrases, blathering on about how delightful it would be to meet again, insist on meeting him in his office.

d) under pressure, smile gently and sadly and explain that no advice can be given until terms have been agreed.

It must be understood that it is a grave mistake to adopt the alternative course of answering questions without comment, and sending in an invoice the next day. The invoice will not be paid.

TACTICS

Objectives

Although consultants are asked to investigate some business problem or other, this is not the real purpose of their involvement. They are not really there to tell people who know a great deal about it how to run their business, something which they are manifestly more informed about than the consultant can ever be. This is merely the surface picture, the ostensible reason for bringing you in.

It is essential for you to grasp at an early stage that the consultant is involved with the client as part of an internal battle. It is extremely likely that two or more courses of action are being debated. Bloody engagements have been fought out across the board-room table. Positions have been adopted by both sides.

The consultant is an additional weapon thrown into the battle, rather as Hitler sent the V1 and V2 rockets to London in a desperate attempt to win World War II. On no account must you make the mistake of supposing that you are the umpire in the contest; you are a participant. The important thing for you, is not to decide what the right course is, but which side is going to win. Prime objectives for the consultant, therefore, are to:

1. Find out what the battle is all about
2. Identify the two sides in the engagement
3. Pin-point the allegiance of all possible participants
4. Decide which is the stronger side
5. Finally, write a report which recommends all the courses which the stronger side favours.

Research

You should constantly bear the following tactical tips in mind:

1. Always do the **basic research** available to all before going to your first meeting with a new client. This is what Reference Libraries are for, as is Companies House, although the latter is today inconveniently placed. Check the biographies of any directors who have made it into *Who's Who*, with special reference to their alleged hobbies. Use *The Directory of Directors* to see if the cast of characters you are dealing with have other irons in the fire.

2. **Balance Sheets** should be studied, especially with a view to discerning what it is they do *not* say. **Company Reports** are unlikely to be absorbing reading, but they must nevertheless be carefully scrutinised, so that the knowledge gained can later be shown off.

3. Never interview anybody with a pre-conceived list of **questions**. Encourage the interviewee to rabbit on. Most business people will chatter away happily about themselves, their manifold responsibilities, how hard they work, their importance in the organisation. The difficulty lies in getting them to stop. But buried in the midst of all their fantasising, there may well be some small nuggets of information, pointers which will help you to work out the true picture.

4. If it is vital to have an accurate record, tape record the event surreptitiously (several pocket recorders have 'conference' settings especially for this); or do it openly if you want to ensure brevity and/or the truth.

Secrecy and Code-words

Large commercial organisations have a strange passion for military terminology. In such enterprises, they tend to talk about 'going on leave' when ordinary human beings would say 'going on holiday'. The reason for this strange quirk has not yet been identified. It may well have something to do with the frustrations which are now inherent in business life. Today the name of the game is persuasion, where once it was a matter of instruction. Perhaps the use of military terms indicates a secret longing for the time when all business was conducted in an authoritarian manner, as it is supposed still happens in the services. Captains of industry secretly harbour a longing to be able to say, like the Centurion in St. Matthew's Gospel: 'I am a man under authority, having soldiers under me; and I say to this man, Go, and he goeth. . .'

This is a mystery. But there is nothing mysterious about the widespread desire, in commerce and industry generally, for secrecy. There are, of course, perfectly sound and sensible reasons for secrecy in business. Plans may be frustrated by rival concerns; if they should get to hear about those plans somebody may get there first.

But the passion for secrecy goes much further than any reasonable bounds. The most likely reason for this is self-importance: secrecy suggests that a man's activities are highly valuable and a possible target for industrial espionage, when in fact they may well be boring and trivial, and of no possible interest to anyone else. Secrecy may also derive from natural deviousness. The man who confides in the consultant probably wishes to keep his activities quiet because his chief object is to do down, or destroy, a colleague. He naturally does not wish to alert this rival and run the risk of letting the other man get his knife in first.

It goes without saying, you must do your best to play up to the widespread longing for secrecy. Indeed you must do your best to outdo the practitioners you meet. Insist on using code-words for firms, people and your own activities. Remembering the requirement for military phraseology, the latter should be referred to as 'Operation X'. Code-words should always be slightly absurd – *Poodle, Pickle, Pumpkin* are good examples. And, for some extraordinary reason, it is customary to use the same initial letter of a man's name when awarding him a code-word; thus Smith becomes *Smug*; Jones, *Junket*; and Robinson, *Rubberband*.

You should also always refuse to use the telephone if the calls are routed through the firm's exchange (a potent source of intelligence). Stipulate the use of private lines. If there are no private lines in the office, insist on calling contacts from home.

All written material should be hand delivered, by a threatening figure in motorcycle gear who demands receipts and only hands over packages personally to the addressee. Everything should be labelled 'Private and Confidential' and sealed with sealing wax.

Jargon

Skilled bluffers do more than familiarise themselves with the jargon of the trade they are connected with at any one time. The jargon changes constantly, as expressions come in and drop out of fashion, but it is not hard to keep abreast of these changes, since the essence of jargon is that it is the language or patois which is in constant use. New words are bandied about by all and sundry as soon as they catch on, so it is only necessary to keep your ears open for this elementary stuff.

Expert consultants do more than this: **they invent their own jargon**. They use words in a way which nobody has heard before, or conjure up a new word, thus underlining once again separateness from their clients. The consultant is not only a creature from another world, he actually *speaks* a different language.

The technique for inventing jargon is simple enough. The trick is to take a noun in common use, and turn it into a verb; or, to reverse the procedure. Loathsome, but impressive-sounding words emerge in this barbarous manner. Profit can spawn 'profitalise'; merchandising can develop 'merchandisation'. And so on. The humble words 'up' and 'down' can be joined with other words in new, surprising and revolting ways e.g. 'In this way, we can seek to up-bottom-line.'

Making Use of Networks

It is impossible to over-emphasise the importance to top management of **secretaries**, or personal assistants as they are more commonly called today. You must spend much time and effort infiltrating the top-management secretarial network of the firm where you are currently working. These women are magnificent allies, all the more so as they are by no means over-worked since they often have their own assistant to deal with mundane chores. They are fearsome adversaries.

The network is supremely well-informed. In really big organisations the top secretaries have their own 'mess' or lunch-club. Given disobliging nicknames,

such as 'Hen-House' and 'Witches Coven', it is a place
to which casual invitations are never issued, but is by
far the best source of intelligence in the whole set-up.

In many ways this group runs the company. Directors and Managers can come and go, but the secretarial
network remains.

These paragons can be enormously helpful to you. It
is, as an example, not merely that each of them can
accurately predict what their boss's views will be on
any possible issue, they can in practice arrange to get
him out of the way, if that is what is required at any
moment. Their network is keenly aware of the power
and influences within the organisation, with all small
details and nuances docketed. It is accordingly to be
cultivated with the greatest care. It can make or break
your entire efforts.

Just as you must do your best to get on to the best
of terms with the key members of the secretarial
network, so too must you do your best to establish
the closest possible relationship with one of the most
important people in the office; namely, **the telephone
switchboard operator**, who often doubles with the
equally important role of **receptionist**.

In the company structure she bridges the gap
between the management secretarial network and the
pseudo-servant group of chauffeurs and go-fers. She
has a foot in both the camps that she straddles; nobody
is in a position to offend her. This is, in consequence,
an unrivalled source of intelligence and information,
with its all-hearing ear casually applied to conver-
sations at the inaudible flick of a switch.

The telephonist and her deputies are often in close
alliance (or alternatively in constant unarmed combat)
with **the mail-room** whose occupant or occupants have
the task of taking in the mail, distributing it around

the place and collecting it later in the day. The person who does this is a vital functionary, in the same way as is the telephone girl. This is literally so, because the absence of either for half a day will cause far more confusion than if the top management departed in a body for a week's fishing.

Another source of intelligence in those offices large enough to boast one, is the man who goes all round the building every afternoon selling evening papers, who always knows all there is to know, invariably before anybody else.

Collectively this team has the vital function of espionage. You must become their Control. Their gossip network is unrivalled, and must at all costs be penetrated. They must be enlisted and milked of information about the power structure of the office. Waste no time; entertain each one of them at the first possible opportunity. Two double-gins usually does the trick. In this way you can save yourself hours, days, even weeks of work. You are dealing with the equivalent of the C.I.A.

Meetings

Desirable though it is to avoid them, meetings are sometimes inescapable. You may indeed find yourself dealing not with an individual, but a Committee or a Working Party. This is unfortunate. Special methods are therefore required to deal with the situation. The technique is simple enough, but the means to put it into effect do need a little effort on your part.

Before the Committee has its first meeting, you will have identified **the person who matters**. This is the one with whom you will work. It is his or her interests which you are furthering. The two of you make up a partnership. In practice, this partnership will make all the decisions apparently made by the Committee. Lip-service has of course to be paid to the Committee. It is an important part of the consultant's job to ensure that nothing detrimental to the interests of the part-nership ever occurs at the meetings of the Committee.

It is your job to find out which side each man, or woman, is on. The best way of doing this is to raise a trivial but contentious issue. For instance, whether the Committee should hold its meetings on a Wednesday. Get the 'senior partner' to express his views first, and then see which way each member decides. This estab-lishes, as it were, their party allegiance.

When this has been done, it remains essential to discover and record the future movements of all those involved, such as:

a) when they are going to be away on trips
b) when they are going on holiday
c) when they are going to be involved in other meetings.

With this information duly plotted and collated, it is a simple matter to arrange for all Committee meetings to be held at times when the opposition will be at its weakest, or even non-existent, and when the partner-ship, with its allies, will be present in force.

While there are still neutral or uncommitted members on the Committee a golden rule to follow is that absolutely anybody will agree to almost anything on the day before they go away on holiday, or leave the office for an overseas trip. On these occasions, even the most sophisticated will be in a mild state of euphoria; they can be relied on to say 'yes' to anything.

Table-Turning

If you are obliged to go to a meeting round a conference table, without time for preparatory work, then precise judgement is needed about which position to take to ensure that the meeting develops as desired. If your judgement is that the Chairman of the meeting is well-disposed to you, then it is sound policy, and will be thought of as the most natural thing, if you sit yourself down next to the Chairman.

If, on the other hand, you have the misfortune to find yourself attending a meeting at which you know or suspect the Chairman to be hostile, then the best course is to position yourself directly opposite him or her, a place that is likely to be at the foot, as opposed to the head of the table, as though you were the hostess at a dinner party at which the Chairman represents the host.

From this position, and only from this position in these circumstances, is it possible for you to dominate the proceedings should they take an unfortunate turn and you are constrained to exert yourself.

This table-turning technique is sometimes known as 'doing a Maxwell' as it is supposed to have been employed by Robert Maxwell on occasions when he attended meetings at which he was not himself in the chair. You may well not be similarly equipped with ample size, vast voice and powerful presence. Nor are you in a position to quell opposition by shouting it down or talking over it. So, cunning and guile are your best weapons. If things are not going your way you must stage diversions, throw spanners in the works, introduce red herrings, create confusion, and do your best to prevent any decisions being taken.

A curiosity of meetings lies in the universal principle of squatter's rights. If the meeting breaks up, perhaps for lunch, and then re-assembles, it will be found that all present have a lemming-like determination to re-occupy the seats they were sitting in before the interruption. If it is to be a table-turning meeting, you cannot do better than to nip in first and blandly occupy the Chairman's seat.

Dealing With People

As he goes about his business, the bluffer will do well to make up his mind about the potential capacities of those he encounters in the world of business and commerce. This is best illustrated by the German army.

It is universally agreed by those who encountered this organisation that it was enormously competent. The methods by which it selected its officers are distinctly instructive. It can and should be studied with profit.

At the completion of each officer-training course, cadets at its schools were divided into four categories. Only two decisions were made about each cadet:

1. They were either clever or they were stupid.
2. They were either lazy or they were hard-working.

It was taken for granted that all of them were brave and had a great sense of responsibility.

Of the four categories, the lazy and stupid cadets were drafted to infantry batallions. The lazy and clever batch were immediately sent on for training as General Staff officers, on the grounds that clever and idle men always find the quickest way of getting things done. The clever and hard-working cadets were despatched for training as Administrative Staff officers, where their qualities were exactly those required in that exacting branch of the service.

This left only one category to be dealt with, the stupid and hard-working ones. And what happened to them? They were returned to civilian life.

As for dealing with business women, whether a consultant is male or female the only thing to learn is that it is a mistake to treat those who have graduated from the tough school of the secretarial world into the realms of management, as if they still were secretaries. What you have to do is to *treat them as men*.

Going Overseas

It will be the aim of all successful, experienced and skilful consultants to talk themselves into making an overseas tour of agencies or branches of any company he or she is dealing with. This is always the icing on the cake, and such an eventuality is very rare indeed, if only for the reason that the top management of any business has firmly held views about such trips, which in practice amount to a rule (unwritten but none the less powerful) that they are the preserve of top management alone.

In consequence it is likely that if you travel abroad you will be sent to the Third World on a consultancy funded by, say, the World Bank, or UNESCO, or some such organization. This is a different proposition, and needs a somewhat different approach from the procedures you will have perfected in the United Kingdom. (Do not consider consulting in or into China or any Soviet state. They expect total competence, on time, and get quite nasty about bluff of any kind.)

The briefing which the consultant gets in London will be at second, or third, hand. It will be virtually useless to you in your search for the elements of the situation which are most important: i.e. what the problem is about, who the disputants are and, most important, whether any advice is really necessary.

There will be a local briefing when you arrive, perhaps by the local resident representative of the World Bank, but this needs to be treated with the utmost caution. Not only are all international organizations like the World Bank riddled with office politics and intrigue, but the resident representative will almost certainly be contaminated by other interests – interests such as:

a) tribal affiliations
b) family links (e.g. relations who are suppliers or shareholders)
c) a political party, in the rare cases where there is more than one political party.

It is obvious that pitfalls and booby traps abound. But you may remain sane and live to tell the tale if you follow three golden rules:

1. Be more than usually discreet, hermetically so.
2. Be very prudent.
3. Be endlessly patient.

All of which are possible provided you listen to all concerned and go on listening until your ears have been bent to a degree where a glimmer of the true position begins to emerge.

The necessary patience is greatly assisted by having no idea of time, apart from reference to the position of the sun. The Third World big-wigs with whom you will be dealing have, generally speaking, none of the

British, or European, obsession with time and timing. They are all too apt to treat time with the contempt which it most probably deserves. The bluffer can outdo and outwit them all by having no watch – if necessary leaving it behind. The absence of a watch has an extraordinarily calming effect. Time ceases to matter. The nerves are soothed, nerves which are all too apt to be frayed in other ways, such as by heat or dust, or other assaults upon the senses. The absence of a watch also destroys at a stroke the normal Third World caricature of an Englishman; this is a red-faced man in an ill-fitting bush shirt and rumpled shorts who constantly and obsessively refers to his wrist-watch.

The sad truth is that the consultant in reality, can do little on these forays. In the two or three weeks you have at your disposal, you can only hope to begin to peel off the outer layer of the onion. It is all too likely that you may be forced into the unwonted and uncomfortable position of having to set out your own real views in the report you will have to present, which is a much more dicey affair than simply presenting the views of the most powerful faction. It is therefore worth noting these elementary points:

a) Be paid before you report. The truth is not always treasured.
b) Be paid by a third party (preferably the World Bank) to whom the number of noughts on the cheque is academic.
c) Be paid in Europe. If hard currency gets into the Third World en route, it may never get out again.
d) Do not discuss barter. It takes an awful lot of peanuts per hour.
e) Do not be paid in gold if you have to smuggle it out.

f) Leave the country *before* you report.

Happily, however, your fee is liable to be large, and the subsistence allowances which are the norm in this sort of work are set at high levels. Trips like these can be very worthwhile.

The Importance of Anecdotes

The consultant does well to equip himself with a good supply of anecdotes about business. These can be trotted out, in conversation, in a knowing way.

It does not do, of course, to hint that you were involved, for example, in the clandestine activities with which Henry Ford II seized power with the connivance of the US Government; this occurred during the last War and it will not help your image to suggest that you were active in business at the time. But it can be delicately suggested that the inside story is only known to such experts as yourself, even though, in fact, you read all about the episode in the *Reader's Digest* in your dentist's waiting room.

There are not all that many sources for rewarding or revealing anecdotes about current, or recent, business. As they are not always creditable to the powers-that-be, they do not appear in company histories – which is the main reason this genre is usually so boring to read. This is why you should store every story for recounting with aplomb at any and every occasion.

A Supreme Bluffer
One of the best and most expert bluffers one could encounter was James G. He is the hero of this anec-

dote, and an example to us all.

Rather more than thirty years ago, James was sitting in the Savoy Grill, then a favourite place for business entertaining in London, waiting for a luncheon companion. At this time the best-known businessman in London was Charles Clore, the aptly-named inventor of the take-over bid, reviled and feared in more or less equal proportions.

James saw, also sitting waiting for a companion to show up, none other than the famous, or infamous, Mr Clore. Never one to waste an opportunity, James approached him.

"Mr Clore," he said "you have no idea who I am. My name is James G. I am here today to give lunch to a man I very much wish to impress. We will be sitting near to the door of the restaurant. Nothing will impress my guest more than your stopping at my table, as you leave, to tap me on the shoulder and say 'Hello, James, how are you?'. If you do this, it will help me enormously."

"Young man," replied Clore "you are a cheeky young fellow. But I rather like cheek. I will do as you say. The best of luck to you."

In due course, all transpired as arranged. Charles Clore stopped at James's table and said his piece. Only to get the reply "Piss off, Charlie, can't you see I'm busy. . ."

44

SPECIALIST CONSULTANTS

Real consultants, as opposed to bluffers, tend to specialise. It is desirable to know something about them, but not to emulate them. There is a sharp gulf between consultants in the older professions and those in new fields of expertise. For examples of the former you need only look to consultant psychiatrists, consultant physicians and so forth. (The rule of thumb is that if they call themselves consultant something they are old school and respectable.) For examples of the latter, try:

Communications consultant	(PR hack)
Search consultant	(headhunter)
Employment consultant	(employment agency interviewer)
Energy consultant	(central heating sales rep)
Education consultant	(encyclopaedia sales rep)
Energy conservation consultant	(double-glazing sales rep)

In other words, the term consultant is almost exclusively self-applied by people who know they are *not* in a profession. The first recorded instance of anyone seeking consultancy advice is in the Garden of Eden. It is perhaps unfortunate for the image of the sector that the snake was the one giving it.

It is not easy for a bluffer to be a specialised consultant, even occasionally, although it is easier occasionally than full-time. This is because their clients expect, need, want and demand results. They will forgive qualified ignorance in a part-time expert but, as with company doctors, salvation and omniscience are preferred. It follows that in this role you would reverse most of the guidelines given in this book. Except those governing fees and payments. Even the consultant's two professional bodies – the Management Consultants Association for firms and the Institute of Management Consultants for individuals – frowns on 'no success, no pay'.

Clients are expected to understand that they are paying for 'consultant time', not for results. The profession sticks firmly to this principle, not least because perfect recommendations implemented by imperfect client's employees will often achieve wholly useless or even negative results. Thus consultants who actually implement cost a lot more, and with good reason.

Consultants of any kind, but particularly the specialist ones, are encouraged to take to heart the following small tale.

The Wise Old Owl

A wee mouse was walking through the wide, wild wood when a wicked wind whipped away his coat, which blew into the branches of a high beech tree. In desperation the mouse sought the advice of a benevolent owl who lived nearby. He told the owl his trouble and the owl said, "No problem. All you have to do is fly up to the branch, loosen the coat and fly down again." The mouse pointed out that he could not fly, to which the owl replied, "Don't bother me with details. I'm a consultant, not a manager."

RECOMMENDATIONS

The essence of consultancy is simply stated, and you should never fail to bear it in mind. You are there to do the dirty work.

Somebody, perhaps the boss, but possibly merely a would-be boss, knows perfectly well what needs to be done. He has taken you on to put what he wants to do into words in the form of recommendations in a report.

He has done this, in part, because your report will appear to the uninitiated to be impartial, and will carry far more weight than the same recommendations if made by himself or any other of the participants involved (in exactly the same way that a report in a newspaper, leaked to that paper by a Minister of the Crown will carry far more weight than the same statement if made by that Minister).

He has also called you in so that he can shelter behind your report and thereby:

1. Reduce the flak that arises from making unpopular changes (i.e. *any* changes).
2. Avoid the odium which comes from sacking people.
3. Evade exposing the viciousness of his feeling for a deadly rival.

It is therefore essential you never make the elementary mistake of supposing for a single moment that any of your careful recommendations will necessarily be put into effect. To believe that is to misunderstand the true nature of the consultancy business.

Nevertheless, it will be necessary to **recommend**, so here are six areas to dabble in; and if what is suggested seems somewhat superficial, do not be concerned. There are real consultants out there winging it on little more than this.

47

1. Titles

Recommendations can be sweetened and made more acceptable if the new structures which are suggested provide a lot of people with appointments which have better-sounding names.

Remember that names and titles cost nothing, but that each title and appointment means a very great deal to the holder of the position.

The magic word Director can easily be incorporated in job-titles which will give great pleasure, but which do not necessarily mean anything very much: Associate Director and Assistant Director are examples of the sort of thing that you should suggest.

Many other useful words can be introduced into the company structure – 'supervisory' is always appreciated as is 'co-ordinator'. The principle to remember is that it pays handsomely and costs nothing to improve people's self-esteem by giving their job a more impressive-sounding title, which nearly always means lengthening it: Supervisory Security Co-ordinator sounds a great deal better than commissionaire or doorman.

2. Employees (At the Top)

Be wary about suggesting an increased number of directors. The Managing Director, Chairman or Board of Directors for whom you are working will certainly regard any suggestion of this kind as crass. These are the last people in the world who will countenance their own devaluation and adulteration by a watering-down of their own status.

There is only one way in which you can with impunity recommend the creation of Directors. This is when you suggest turning a department or a division of the concern into a subsidiary company. Or several subsidiary companies. This has the great merit of pleasing all concerned. The Directors of the subsidiary companies will be delighted at their own new status; the original Board of Directors will be equally delighted, as they automatically become Main Board Directors. They are not threatened by the change; on the contrary, their position is enhanced, and their standing increased. They may even be able to thin their own ranks judiciously, by leaving colleagues out of favour in situ, as it were, by relegating them to the lower, subsidiary Board.

Employees (At the Bottom)

A very important group of people surrounds top management of large companies (and indeed some quite small companies), apart from the secretarial staff and the personal assistants, and is separate from the main business hierarchy. This group consists of chauffeurs, doormen, waiters, cooks and butlers in management dining rooms, and others whose function is to make the management more comfortable. Consultants must be very wary indeed of making any recommendations affecting this group. To do so is to play with fire in the most dangerous possible way.

It goes without saying that many in this category of employee are absurdly under-employed, often wholly so. It is perfectly possible for a chauffeur to work for less than a couple of hours a day for weeks on end, although this is not to say that he may also have to work occasionally what are supposed to be unsocial hours, for which he is suitably rewarded. All this waste of effort, or lack of effort, is justified as saving management time.

Many in this group were recruited direct from the Armed Forces. There they acquired not only the 'clean conduct sheet' which is still a passport to this kind of job in the first place, but the art, perfected by many generations of Non-Commissioned Officers, of skiving, that is to say appearing to be hard at work when actually doing less than nothing at all. They are adept at melting into the background, and can even disappear with Lewis Carroll-like facility. Without exception, members of this group are gossips and know-alls, no doubt because they have many hours at their disposal when there is little to do except talk to each other.

One of the functions of the group, in fact their chief reason for existence, is to feed management illusions. They boost management self-respect by treating them with old-fashioned respect and deference. If a Managing Director supposes that he is on pleasant terms of familiarity with his chauffeur, he is all too liable to suffer from the illusion that he is thereby in touch with the views and opinions of 'the shop floor'. Nothing could be further from the truth. All chauffeurs are by nature sycophants; moreover, they are, like taxi-drivers, right-wing to a man; and they only talk to other chauffeurs, and others in their group.

Managers, whose home life is much the same as anybody else's, have their egos massaged by being cossetted in their offices by this group of employees, who have all the appearance and manner of personal servants. In practice, the 'dear old boy' who performs as the butler in the directors' private dining suite at Head Office, does indeed sometimes put in an appearance in the same role at the Managing Director's dinner parties at his home, thereby extending the illusion.

A sensible consultant leaves this group severely alone. Any changes whatever to their functions or responsibilities will be thought to be a bad thing – bad for the management and in consequence bad for you.

3. Plausibility

In commercial organisations of every kind, apart from the smallest, much time and effort is expended in seeking to find plausible reasons for pursuing a course which people in authority want to take either because:

a) they simply want to do it (for no particular reason, just a gut feeling)

b) the real reasons are unworthy, if not downright dishonest.

No retail organisation, for example, would dream of saying that it has plans to open a branch in a particular provincial town because it would be a great convenience for the Chairman's current mistress. The branch will no doubt be opened, after some straight-faced, or mercifully ignorant, expert has made a presentation of all the compelling commercial reasons why that branch should be opened at that particular time.

Again, offices can be moved for ostensibly sound commercial reasons (lower rent, better address, better facilities, more space, less space, etc.) when in fact the Managing Director merely wants to reduce the time it takes him to get to his club and back again at lunchtime.

It is much the same with diversification. A firm that is and has done well for years in its own field, often supposes that it could do equally well in another area of commerce, not related to the original one. The powers-that-be almost certainly want to embark on this risky course because they are bored with what they have been doing so successfully for so many years. It is and has long been all too easy, and they look for the excitement which the new venture will bring into their lives. But nobody would dream of giving utterance to these secret longings – the new venture will be dressed up with all the paraphernalia of commercial wisdom, reports, appraisals, studies and so on. Plausibility has to be achieved.

It is easy enough for you to help provide the respectable reasons for doing what is wanted. The difficulty lies in finding out what is really wanted, something which is rarely put into words on any occasion.

It is no great secret that in the world of business rivalries are often pursued with great vigour. Colleagues who treat each other with breezy camaraderie ('How's your good lady?') are often bitter rivals under this surface veneer. Two men, let us say, both want the top job in the business when the present incumbent retires, as he is due to do in two years' time. Part of your job as a consultant is to provide respectable clothing to mask this vendetta. You will have already selected your man, that is to say, the one who is going to emerge triumphant; it is up to you to suggest ways of doing down, perhaps even ways of getting rid of, the rival. Such as:

1. Putting the person in charge of an already doomed subsidiary company (the classic method).
2. Inventing a new appointment which sounds grand, but is in fact powerless, and promoting (note the position is always up, never down) the rival to this post, effectively emasculating him or her in a commercial House of Lords.

Nobody ever spells out such matters. It is all done with nods and winks. The consultant has to be a skilled interpreter of these, as of the pregnant silence.

4. Profitability

It is the most natural thing in the world for business people to suppose that if their profits are satisfactory, there is little else to worry about. All public comment and most business training suggests that this is the case. 'The bottom line' as they say, is what matters, and seems to matter to the exclusion of everything else.

The consultant needs to be very well aware that this is a short-sighted view. Suppose that there is a group of companies, with a number of uneven-sized concerns in the group. Suppose, further, that the smallest of these companies (with a turnover of £2M) has and is making losses (£80,000 last year, £50,000 this year). Fur will certainly be flying; heads will roll or have rolled. Every possible effort is made to right this situation, with an inordinate amount of top-management time being used.

All of which ignores the fact, unrevealed by the figures, that one of the larger companies in the group, which has a turnover of £15M and what are thought to be satisfactory profits of £1.5M, is very sleepily managed and could, with quite minor changes, and very little cost, increase its profits by not less than £¾M a year.

The consultant ought not to take a straight-forward, accountancy view of things. The balance sheet and the profit and loss accounts tell you something, but cannot tell you all. You should look beyond and behind the figures, to find the most attractive pasture to browse in.

5. Foreign Travel

The consultant does well to make use of the fact that business people actually *like* foreign travel. They do not, of course, put this into words, because they suppose that enthusiasm for foreign travel will sound juvenile and unsophisticated. Besides, as travel is one of the prerequisites of top management, they want to keep it to themselves. They will endlessly stress the horrors they are supposed to have encountered, seeking to ensure that their underlings do not even suspect that the trips are remotely enjoyable.

The ordinary person, accustomed to and conditioned by the rigours of the package tour from Luton Airport, the hideous surroundings, the sardine-tin ambience, the plastic food and the endless unexplained delays, has small difficulty in accepting the Chairman's lurid description of his hold-up in Bahrein. '120 degrees,' he says, omitting to mention that he was never out of air-conditioned rooms.

Ordinary people, likewise, have very little concept of the comforts and delights provided for the first-class passenger; nor can they visualise, for example, the Mandarin Hotel in Hong Kong, which is certainly a very far cry from the upended matchbox in Benidorm where so many last saw the inside of a foreign, indeed any, hotel.

By suggesting a course of action which implies regular overseas trips, you will present the chosen few with the opportunity for regular delightful holidays.

Blandness is all. When making the suggestion on which all this is based, such as the imperative need to open a Branch Office in the Far East, you must shake your head mournfully. Say, as lugubriously as you can, "But I fear that this recommendation carries with it the grave disadvantage that you yourself will have to go there – I suppose annually – to keep an eye on things. I would not of course suggest this course, if I did not think it absolutely essential; because, as I am sure you know, trips of that kind are most exhausting and time-consuming, all the more so as most people at your level find the whole thing so wearing that they find it essential to take a bit of a break on the way home – I believe that Thailand is one of the favoured places."

Another reason for the popularity of foreign travel, most compelling but never referred to, is best illustrated by an anecdote about a young Japanese businessman. He had been told that he would have to leave his Tokyo Head Office for a trip around the world, lasting six weeks. It was made quite clear to him that this was in part a reward for his many achievements and services. All preparations were made. Unfortunately, two weeks before he was due to set off, he committed some terrible solecism, incomprehensible to a Westerner, but a grave mistake in Japan, especially for an ambitious and aspiring young man. He was summoned to his Chairman's office. He expected, at the very least, to be told the trip was cancelled; transfer to Korea was a possibility; even hara kiri loomed. But his punishment was different: he was told that it had been decided that his wife would accompany him on his trip.

6. Surroundings

Never underestimate the importance, to the individual, of his own place of work, the particular slot in which he works in the beehive that surrounds him.

People get extraordinarily attached to the precise

spot in which they carry out their daily tasks – their room, their cubby-hole, their desk. As far as they can, they seek to make this corner a second home, decorating it with rubber-plants, photographs, pasting up calendars, and in other ways trying to identify the place with their own individuality. The less they are paid, the more tedious their work, the more this is true. One of the features of the open-plan office is that it goes a long way towards destroying the possibilities for individualising the work-place. Intended to be more flexible, and consequently in a constant state of flux, the denizens of the open-plan office are less able to get dug into their own corner. Change is the name of the game, and they are conditioned to it.

It is not altogether surprising that people develop passionate attachments to their individual place of work. Years ago it was not at all infrequent for people to spend as much as one third of the hours of the week at their office desks or workbench; today the figure is unlikely to be above one quarter. But in terms of people's self-esteem these are very important hours. Thus changes of any kind which in any way involve alterations to the surroundings in which people work are inevitably highly unpopular.

If such changes have to be made, they have to be approached with care, so that an unpleasantly explosive situation is avoided. You will, of course, ensure that you yourself are not too closely identified with the changes. It may well be possible to arrange matters so that a key opposition figure is landed with the harrowing job of putting the changes into effect – thus putting him or her into the firing-line, the ploy invented by King David with Uriah the Hittite. If chaos is not to follow, somebody with sufficient authority has to sell the changes before they are made, and then slap down all the efforts which will certainly follow, in which individuals seek to have exceptions made for themselves, to adulterate the plans, and sabotage your suggestions.

Further up the hierarchy, the problem takes a rather different form. Here you will find members of the management team will view any change, such as a move of offices, or a reshuffle of offices, as a golden opportunity to increase their own apparent status. They hope to get a bigger, or better-situated, or better-decorated office for themselves. They will politic vigorously to achieve the most modest of improvements in the surroundings and the fittings which reflect their status among their colleagues, and rivals, in the long-running, indeed continuously-running saga of the fight for promotion and advancement.

THE REPORT

The consultant's **Report** is of paramount importance. It is the only thing you leave behind with the company when you go on your way. Skilled bluffers, which may be taken to include all serious students of the present work, will of course recognise that nobody is going to read all through the Report. The most that can be expected is that those for whom it is intended will glance at **the summary** of the recommendations. But this by no means lets you off the hook; the Report must be made to look tremendously impressive.

This is not only because the consultant's ample fee must be matched by a weighty-looking Report, though this in itself is sufficient reason to spend much time and energy putting the Report together, but because people like to feel that they are getting something worthwhile for their money. A more compelling reason is that the Report, if it looks sufficiently impressive, will be used by the company to impress others – colleagues and business associates. It is a vital form of advertising for you.

Appearance

Presentation is all-important. The thing should be impeccably word-processed, with much use of space and margins. It should be carefully reproduced, if possible by the in-house printing set-up. Sections of different-coloured papers can be used to good effect. There should be a proper cover to the Report, which should be held together by a plastic ring-binding. As usual, you must guard against getting carried away with natural enthusiasm – a morocco leather binding, for example, is too extravagant.

Size

The contents of the Report are of much less importance than its appearance. Bulk is what is required. In part this can be achieved by repeating everything three times, a technique practised by all the most effective communicators, from the Prophet Mohammed to Goebbels, whose motto was 'What I tell you three times is true'.

Not only repetition is needed. The analysis section of the Report should be boosted by an avalanche of facts, charts, diagrams and lists of doubtful relevance. These can be ancient history, and simply lifted from any available source, such as old company reports. It does not matter in the least that all this material will be totally familiar to all those for whom it is ostensibly intended – there is no chance at all that they will wade through this morass. If all else fails, and invention flags, you can easily bung in page after page of official government or European Comunity statistics, however irrelevant. Weight and weightiness are the sole requirement.

Quantity

The Report should be produced in far larger numbers than can possibly be needed, to ensure that your name is given maximum circulation. Two hundred copies is the proper minimum, but you should never ask anybody about the quantity, just blandly have them done.

Each one should, of course, be individually numbered and labelled **Top Secret**.

Contents

Reports should normally consist of the following sections:

— introduction
— description of the consultant's brief
— the historical background
— analysis of the current situation
— the reasoning behind the recommendations
— summary of the recommendations

The only section to which any attention will be paid is the last, which is why it is often placed first, to make it easy to find.

Embellishments

When writing a report, never waste time seeking out a telling quotation. Go for industrial and commercial sages such as Peter Drucker. These are much to be recommended since they add respectability to what is otherwise, in all probability, a collection of common sense. Moreover, Drucker has written so much, all of it very sensible, that it is a simple matter to take a chunk of his prose, almost at random, and shove it in at the head of a section or chapter, where its relevance or irrelevance will pass unnoticed. If you do manage to get it right, and turn up a relevant quote, it certainly says more in a sentence than you will achieve in a whole chapter.

But there is an even craftier device; this is to quote Chinese sages. Here the bluffer should follow the admirable example of H. W. Tilman, the tough mountaineer and explorer. He it was who when describing the experience of scaling a phenomenally difficult peak said, 'We so far forgot ourselves as to shake hands.' When stuck for a quote, for example, to justify his detestation of scientists and other hangers-on to expeditions which, in his view, should simply have consisted of people who wanted to go, he would often quote the sayings of anonymous Chinese wise men. They were always anonymous because Tilman invariably extemporised the sayings himself.

You should be able to do this sort of thing without a moment's hesitation, expressions such as: "He who hurls stones in greenhouses does not deserve central heating" or "He who pisses in the ocean deserves not good tomatoes."

Essentials

It is a wise precaution to make recommendations which will produce foreseeable savings large enough to exceed and outweigh your handsome fees and expenses.

It does not do to spell out the equation in your Report – such blatant methods may well prove counter-productive. But it is advisable and prudent to refer to the savings which will accrue if your recommendations are followed. The powers-that-be can be relied on to spell out the comparison for themselves – this is the sort of arithmetic they understand.

In this way you do your best to ensure that you will be invited back again to the same company to deal with another, or supposed problem, in the future.

THE AUTHOR

Nigel Viney, having bluffed his way through a fruitful career in book publishing (with an interval in the oil industry) is now enjoying a new career as a Consultant. He insists his success in this field is solely because he realised at once that Consultancy is populated exclusively by bluffers, the most triumphant being those who succeed in bluffing themselves as effectively as their clients.

Nigel Viney is only prepared to reveal all, in this Bluffer's Guide, because he is now well launched on a third career as a writer, having published several books about words, the writer's raw material. These include *Magenta Marathon Mecca*, a glossary of toponyms, and *Amontillado to Yorkshire Pudding*, a glossary of personal and place names in food and drink, subjects which, like Consultancy, are ever in demand.

THE BLUFFER'S GUIDES®

Available at £1.99 and *£2.50 each:

Accountancy*
Advertising*
Antiques
Archaeology*
Astrology & Fortune Telling
Ballet
Bluffing*
British Class
Champagne*
Chess*
Classics*
Computers*
Consultancy*
Cricket
Doctoring*
European Union*
Finance*
Flight Deck
Golf*
Japan
Jazz*
Journalism
Literature
Management*
Marketing*
Maths

Modern Art
Motoring
Music*
Occult
Opera*
Paris*
Philosophy*
Photography
Poetry
P.R.
Public Speaking
Publishing
Races*
Rugby*
Science*
Secretaries
Seduction*
Sex*
Skiing*
Small Business*
Teaching*
Theatre
University*
Weather
Whisky
Wine*

All these books are available at your local bookshop or newsagent, or by post or telephone from: B.B.C.S., P.O.Box 941, Hull HU1 3VQ.

UK (& BFPO) Orders: £1.00 for the first book & 50p for each additional book up to a maximum of £2.50;
Overseas (& Eire) Orders: £2.00 for the first book, £1.00 for the second & 50p for each additional book.

(24 hour Telephone Credit Card Line: 01482 224626).